CATS
of the
WILD

CHEETAHS

Henry Randall

PowerKiDS press™

New York

Published in 2011 by The Rosen Publishing Group, Inc.
29 East 21st Street, New York, NY 10010

First Edition

Editor: Joanne Randolph
Book Design: Ashley Burrell

Photo Credits: Cover, pp. 13, 24 (right) Shutterstock.com; pp. 5, 24 (center right) © www.iStockphoto.com/Peter Malsbury; pp. 6–7 Andy Rouse/Getty Images; pp. 8–9, 24 (center left) © Paul Goldstein/age fotostock; p. 10 Jupiterimages/Photos.com/Thinkstock; p. 14 iStockphoto/Thinkstock; p. 17 Art Wolfe/Getty Images; pp. 18, 24 (left) Anup Shah/Photodisc/Thinkstock; p. 21 © www.iStockphoto.com/Francois Van Heerden; p. 22 Tom Brakefield/Stockbyte/Thinkstock.

Library of Congress Cataloging-in-Publication Data

Randall, Henry, 1972-
  Cheetahs / by Henry Randall. — 1st ed.
       p. cm. — (Cats of the wild)
  Includes index.
  ISBN 978-1-4488-2518-9 (library binding) — ISBN 978-1-4488-2621-6 (pbk.) — ISBN 978-1-4488-2622-3 (6-pack)
  1. Cheetah—Juvenile literature. I. Title.
  QL737.C23R355 2011
  599.75′9—dc22
                                                2010020813

Manufactured in the United States of America

CPSIA Compliance Information: Batch #WW11PK: For Further Information contact Rosen Publishing, New York, New York at 1-800-237-9932

Contents

Cheetahs are beautiful wild cats. Can you see the **spots** on this cheetah's fur?

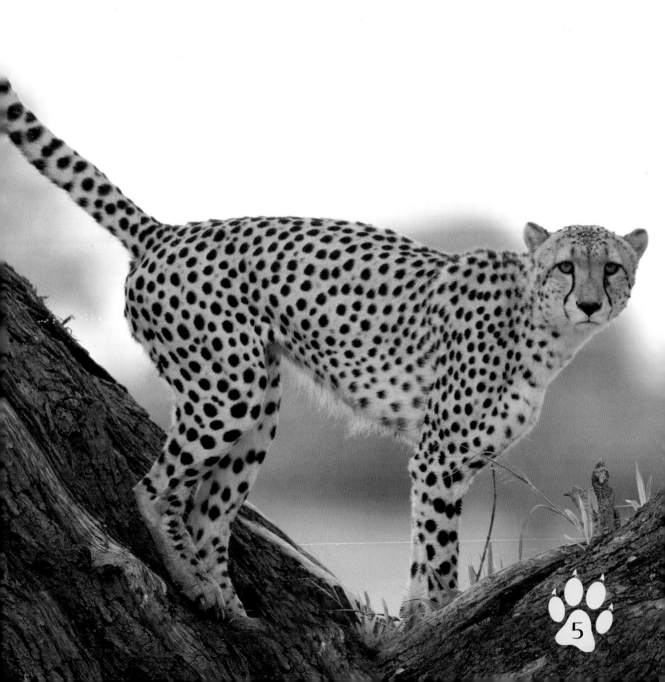

Cheetahs are the fastest animals on land. Their bodies are made to move quickly.

6

Cheetahs live on big, grassy **fields** in Africa. These fields are called savannas.

Savannas do not have many trees. Cheetahs hunt the animals that come to eat the grass there.

Cheetahs are good at climbing. This cheetah looks for food from atop a hill built by **termites**.

This cheetah has climbed
a tree to get a good look
around.

Cheetahs hide in the long grass of the savanna. Can you find the cheetah here?

Cheetah babies are called **cubs**. A cub's fur is softer and longer than its mother's fur.

Male cheetahs may live in small groups. Female cheetahs without cubs live alone.

Cheetahs use their eyes and ears when they hunt. Cheetahs are interesting cats!

Words to Know

cub

field

spots

termites

Index

Web Sites

Due to the changing nature of Internet links, PowerKids Press has developed an online list of Web sites related to the subject of this book. This site is updated regularly. Please use this link to access the list:
www.powerkidslinks.com/cotw/cheetah/